Learning How to Live

Faith Activities for Catholic Kids

Grade 4

Pflaum Publishing Group
Dayton, OH 45439

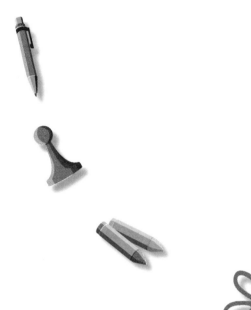

Learning How to Live
Faith Activities for Catholic Kids
Grade 4

Content and design by Victory Productions, Worcester, MA 01609
General Editors: Karen Cannizzo and Cullen Schippe

Nihil obstat: Reverend Monsignor John F. Murphy, *censor librorum*,
May 24, 2005

Imprimatur: † Most Reverend Timothy M. Dolan, Archbishop of Milwaukee,
June 2, 2005

Scripture quotations contained herein are from the *New Revised Standard
Version Bible*: Catholic Edition, © 1993 and 1989 by the Division of Christian
Education of the National Council of the Churches of Christ in the United
States of America. Used by permission. All rights reserved.

Text of morning and evening prayers adapted from *Book of Catholic Prayer*,
Edmund Bliven, ed., Oregon Catholic Press, 1997.

ISBN 1-933178-18-3

Contents

I Believe

I Celebrate

I Follow Jesus

I Pray

God's Promises

On the lines, write two promises you made recently. If you kept the promise, color in the happy face. If you broke the promise, color in the sad face.

1. _____

2. _____

God makes promises, too. But God never breaks a promise. God is always faithful, or true to his promises.

God promises to be with us always. He asks us in return to honor his commandments. This special promise is a sacred agreement called a covenant.

Signs of Covenant

The Bible is full of stories about God's faithfulness to his promises. Signs help us remember these stories. Draw a line from each story to the matching sign of the covenant.

Story   **Sign**

God promised Noah never again to destroy the earth with a flood.

God promised Abraham and Sarah that they would have as many descendants as there are stars in the sky.

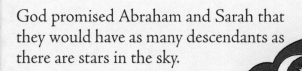

God promised Moses and the Israelites that they would always be his people.

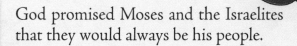

God promised to send his Son, Jesus, to save all people from sin.

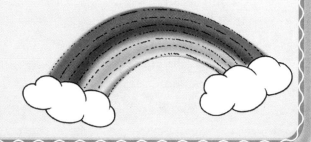

God Speaks to Us

Words, spoken or written, carry powerful messages.

What are the best words you heard someone say to you this week?

_____

What was the best message you ever got in the mail, on the phone, or by e-mail?

_____

God's words carry the most powerful messages of all. God speaks to us in the words of the Bible. The Bible is also called Sacred Scripture, or "holy writing." We also know it as God's Word.

Using the Bible

To find a passage in the Bible, follow these directions.

This word tells you which book of the Bible to find. Look in the table of contents to find the book in your Bible.

This number tells you which chapter of the book to look for. Each chapter begins with a large number, and the top of each page is marked with the chapter number, too.

John 3:16

This punctuation mark separates the chapter number from the number of the verse or verses.

This number tells you which verse, or line of the chapter, to look for. Tiny numbers mark the beginning of each verse.

Find John 3:16 in your Bible. Write this verse here.

_____

_____

_____

_____

Obeying and Disobeying

God asks us to be faithful to the commandments he has given us. The commandments are laws for our relationship with God and with one another.

What is one rule, or law, your family has?

_____

What is one rule, or law, your community has?

_____

A big part of obeying is listening. When you obey, you listen to what others need from you. When you disobey, you don't listen to anyone but yourself. You want things your own way.

The First Disobedience

The Bible tells a story about how the first humans disobeyed God. Their disobedience is known as original sin. Work with a partner to unscramble the words in big blue letters so the story makes sense.

The first humans were named _____ (**MAAD**) and _____ (**VEE**).

God made a beautiful _____ (**RAGNED**) for them to live in and care for.

God gave them free _____ (**LILW**) so they could make their own choices.

"I give you just one rule," God said. "Don't eat the _____ (**TUFIR**) of that one tree over there."

But the sly _____ (**PERSENT**) tempted Eve to _____ (**TEA**) the fruit.

She _____ (**VGEA**) some to Adam, and he ate, too.

Adam and Eve knew they had done _____ (**NOGRW**). They sinned by disobeying God. They didn't _____ (**NESTIL**) because they wanted their own way.

They felt ashamed, and they tried to _____ (**HEDI**) from God.

Consequences

Every choice you make has *consequences*, or things that happen because of your choice. If you choose to make the last packet of instant oatmeal for breakfast, for example, your little brother will have to eat cold cereal. If you choose to wear your red sweater, you can't wear your blue sweater, too.

Write one possible consequence of each of these choices.

Choice	Consequence
You spend all of this week's allowance the day you get it.	_____
You spend Saturday afternoon at the movies instead of cleaning your room.	_____
You sign up for soccer and you make the team.	_____

Good and Evil

Some choices have more serious consequences than others. You can choose to do what is right or to do what is wrong. We call this making a choice between good and evil.

Write one possible consequence of each of these wrong choices.

Choice	Consequence
You break your sister's toy on purpose.	_____
You call your friend a mean name.	_____
You cheat on your math test.	_____

Jesus Saves Us

Even though Adam and Eve made the choice to disobey God, God did not stop loving and caring for them. In fact, original sin had one very good consequence. God promised to send his own Son, Jesus, to save all people.

Overcoming Sin

Jesus came to save us from sin. Following Jesus can help us overcome the consequences of original sin every day.

Because of original sin, humans are tempted to choose what is wrong.	Jesus became human to show us how to say no to temptation.	Write about or draw someone who helps you make good choices.
Because of original sin, suffering and death came into the world.	Jesus suffered and died for us to show us that God's love is stronger than death.	Write a prayer of thanks to Jesus.
Because of original sin, the first humans had to leave the garden God made.	Jesus rose from death and returned to his Father in heaven to show us that we can be happy forever with God.	Write about or draw your idea of heaven.

And that's a fact...

The name *Jesus* is the Greek form of the Aramaic name *Yeshua*. In Hebrew, it's *Joshua*. All these names mean the same thing: "God saves."

A Different Kind of King

Some people were expecting Jesus to come into the world as a great king. They thought he would be rich and powerful. They thought he would change the world by force.

Jesus was a very different kind of king. He was born poor and powerless. He led a small band of close friends, not an army. He changed the world by love.

The Way to the Kingdom

Jesus taught people that God's kingdom was a kingdom of justice, love, and peace. All his life, Jesus showed people the way to God's Kingdom. You can find the way, too. Follow the paths you think Jesus would show you.

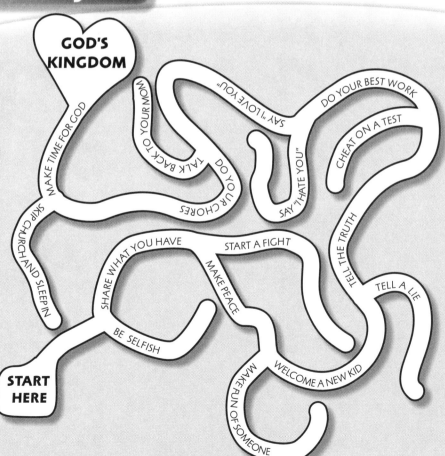

GOD'S KINGDOM

MAKE TIME FOR GOD

TALK BACK TO YOUR MOM

SAY "I LOVE YOU"

DO YOUR BEST WORK

CHEAT ON A TEST

DO YOUR CHORES

SAY "I HATE YOU"

SKIP CHURCH AND SLEEP IN

SHARE WHAT YOU HAVE

START A FIGHT

MAKE PEACE

TELL THE TRUTH

TELL A LIE

BE SELFISH

WELCOME A NEW KID

MAKE FUN OF SOMEONE

START HERE

The Holy Spirit Helps

When Jesus returned to his Father, he did not leave us alone. God's Holy Spirit came to be with the Church. You became a member of the Church in Baptism. This means that the Holy Spirit is with you, too. The Holy Spirit helps you make moral choices—choices between right and wrong.

Make a Pinwheel

Wind and breath are signs of the Holy Spirit. Make a pinwheel to remind you that the Holy Spirit is with you to help you make good choices.

You'll need:
+ 2 six-inch squares of paper, each a different color
+ glue stick
+ crayons or markers
+ scissors
+ a pushpin
+ 1 or 2 small glass beads
+ a pencil with an eraser

1. Glue the two squares of paper together, back to back, so you have one square.

2. Fold your square, corner to corner. Then unfold it again.

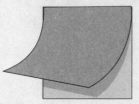

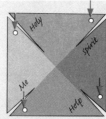

3. Make a mark about 1/3 of the way from the center of each fold line. Put a dot in every other point. Copy the words "Holy Spirit, help me!" onto the other points, as shown here.

4. Cut along the fold lines. Stop at the marks you made.

5. Carefully use the pushpin to poke a hole in each point where there is a dot.

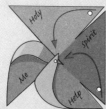

6. Bring every other point (the ones with the holes) to the middle. Don't fold the paper.

7. Carefully push the pin through all four holes and into the center of the pinwheel. Thread a small glass bead onto the end of the pin. Then carefully push the pin (with the pinwheel and the bead) into the pencil eraser.

Hold the pencil and softly blow on the pinwheel. Watch your prayer spin!

Signs of God's Presence

God made a covenant to be with his people always. You can see signs of God's presence everywhere—in a rainbow after a storm, a friend's smile, or your grandma's homemade soup.

Draw a sign of God's presence that you see in nature.

Draw a sign of God's presence that you see in your family.

Draw a sign of God's presence that you see in your community.

Church Signs

When you go to church, you see many reminders of God's presence.

A **crucifix** is an image of Jesus on the cross. This sign reminds you that God sent his Son to save us. You may see a crucifix near the altar in church, or carried in the entrance procession at Mass.

At Mass, the **bread and wine** become the Body and Blood of Christ. You receive Jesus in Holy Communion, a lasting sign that God is with you.

Consecrated hosts are kept safe in a special, decorated cabinet called a **tabernacle.** A candle or lamp burns near the tabernacle as a sign that Jesus is present in the Blessed Sacrament.

Draw one other sign of God's presence that you see in your parish church.

11

We Celebrate Sacraments

The Church celebrates God's presence with us in the sacraments. Sacraments are signs and celebrations of God's presence. We grow in grace through the sacraments. Growing in grace means sharing more and more in God's life.

Catholics celebrate seven sacraments. Do you remember their names? Fill in the missing letters.

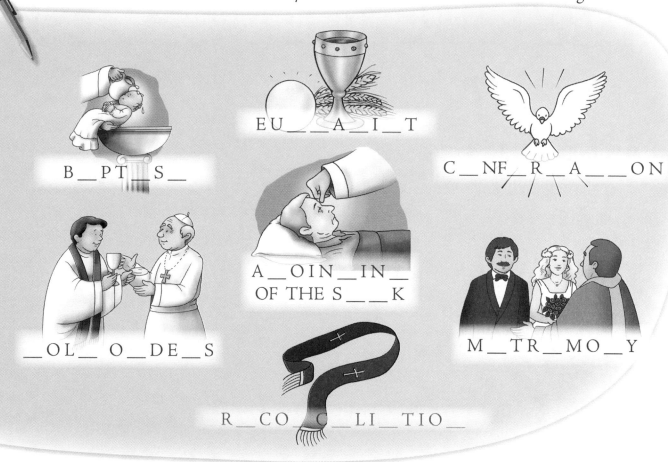

B_ PT__S_

EU__A_I_T

C__NF_R__A___ON

__OL__O__DE__S

A__OIN__IN__
OF THE S___K

M_TR__MO__Y

R__CO__C__LI__TIO_

The Mass

The Eucharist, which is another name for the Mass, is the greatest celebration of God's presence. On a separate sheet of paper, draw your favorite part of the Mass.

And that's a fact...

The name for the prayers and actions of the Mass is *liturgy*. The word *liturgy* means "the work of the people." Everyone has a part to play in celebrating the liturgy. No one is just part of the audience at Mass!

Gathering and Listening

Sunday Mass is a celebration that begins with people gathering together. We gather in church and sing a hymn as the priest and the other participants walk onto the altar.

Write the title of, or a line from, one of your favorite hymns.

_____

We exchange a greeting with the priest. We ask God to forgive our sins as we gather to celebrate the Eucharist. We sing or pray a hymn of praise, and the priest leads us in prayer.

Celebrating the Word

The Liturgy of the Word, the first part of the Mass, reminds us why we are celebrating. In this part of the Mass:

+ We hear God's Word proclaimed from the Bible.
+ We respond with a psalm.
+ We listen as the priest or deacon explains the readings in a homily.
+ We profess our faith in the words of the Nicene Creed.
+ We pray for the needs of all people in the General Intercessions.

Each Sunday has special Bible readings. Do some hunting and find the readings for last Sunday. Then fill in this chart.

Reading	The book, chapter, and verses of the Bible for this reading	One message I got from this reading
First Reading (Old Testament)	_____	_____
Responsorial (Psalm)	_____	_____
Second Reading (New Testament Letter)	_____	_____
Gospel	_____	_____

Remembering and Sharing

To remember something, you use your senses and your imagination. A good memory can be like reliving a wonderful experience again and again.

Think of one of the best meals you remember sharing. Who was there? What did you eat? What made this meal so special?

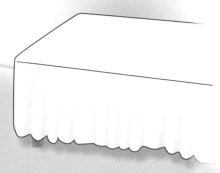

On the table, write or draw things you remember about this wonderful meal.

A Meal and a Sacrifice

You know that Jesus suffered and died to save us from sin. This loving offering of his life was Jesus' sacrifice. Jesus gave us a special way to remember his sacrifice and love for us. At his Last Supper with his friends, Jesus gave us the Eucharist.

In the Liturgy of the Eucharist, we remember and celebrate Jesus' sacrifice on the cross. We share Holy Communion, the meal in which Jesus is truly present.

Find the correct words in the Word Bank to complete the words of Jesus that the priest says during the Eucharistic Prayer.

"Take this, _____ of you, and _____ it:

This is my _____ which will be _____ up for you."

"Take this, all of you, and _____ from it:

This is the _____ of my _____, the blood

of the _____ and everlasting _____.

It will be _____ for you and for all, so that _____

may be _____. Do this in _____ of me."

Word Bank

| all | body | cup | eat | given | memory | shed |
| blood | covenant | drink | forgiven | God | new | sins |

14

Words of Celebration

What would life be like without words? How would you communicate with others? How would you describe what you feel?

When Helen Keller was a baby, she caught a disease that caused her to lose the ability to see and to hear. Helen was locked in a world without words. She was so frustrated by not being able to communicate that she was always angry. She threw temper tantrums.

Then Helen's family found a teacher named Annie Sullivan. Annie taught Helen to "hear" the words that Annie spelled out with her fingers in Helen's palm. Once Helen had words, her world opened up. She became a great writer and teacher.

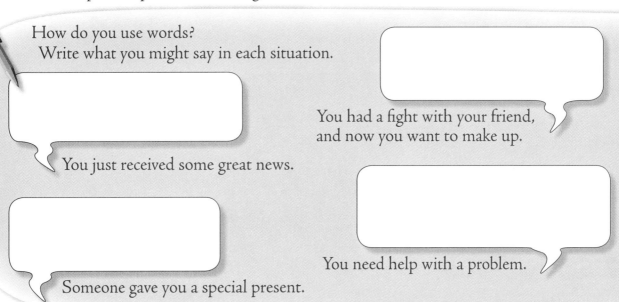

How do you use words?
Write what you might say in each situation.

You just received some great news.

You had a fight with your friend, and now you want to make up.

Someone gave you a special present.

You need help with a problem.

Words at Mass

We use words in the celebration of the Mass to communicate with God and with one another. Read what each of these words or phrases means. The next time you are at Mass, pray or sing these words with feeling.

Words	What They Mean
Lord, have mercy.	God, help me turn away from sin and do better.
Glory to God in the highest . . .	We honor God above all things.
Alleluia!	Praise God!
Christ has died, Christ is risen, Christ will come again.	We believe that Jesus died for us, rose from the dead, and will return at the end of time.
Amen.	Yes, I believe that it is so.
Thanks be to God.	We are grateful for all God's gifts.

Celebrating in Action

You can use your facial expression, the way you stand, and the way you move or gesture to "speak" without words, or to add meaning to the words you speak.

What is each person "saying"?

Body Prayers

You use gestures, actions, and postures as well as words to pray at Mass.
Here are some of these ways you pray with your body.

You make the **Sign of the Cross** with holy water when you enter the church. This action helps you remember your Baptism

You exchange a **sign of peace** with other members of the community to show that we are all united in the Body of Christ.

You **genuflect** (kneel briefly on one knee) as a sign of respect for Jesus present in the Blessed Sacrament.

You **hold out your hands** in a prayerful gesture to receive Jesus in Holy Communion.

To Love and Serve the Lord

Have you ever seen a movie or read a book in which the characters were sent on a mission? Someone with a mission has a special task to do or an important message to share.

With a friend or family member, make up a story about someone who is sent on a mission. Have your story answer these questions.

- Who is the person being sent?
- Who is the sender?
- To what people or place is the person being sent?
- What is the person's mission?

- Who helps the character carry out the mission?
- Does he or she succeed? Why or why not?

Share your story with your family, friends, or classmates.

Your Mission

Did you know that you are sent on a mission every Sunday? At the end of the Mass, the priest or deacon says, "Go in peace to love and serve the Lord." He is sending you on a mission from God. Your mission is to share God's presence and the good news of Jesus with everyone you meet during the week.

Complete each sentence in your own words to tell the story of your mission.

This week, I shared God's love with someone when I _____

_____

This week, I served others by _____

_____

This week, I shared the good news of Jesus by _____

_____

And that's a fact...

Our name for the Eucharist, the Mass, comes from the end of the celebration. *Mass* comes from the Latin word *missa*, which means "sending forth." After every Mass, we are sent forth to show everyone we meet that we are followers of Jesus, and we bring his love to them.

Rules of Love

When you hear the word *rule*, do you think of a *ruler*? You measure inches or centimeters with a ruler. But how do you measure your choices and actions?

Jesus gave his followers a rule they could use to measure the goodness of their deeds. This "moral ruler" is so valuable that we call it the **Golden Rule**. You can use this tool to measure how well you are showing love in your everyday life.

> ## "In everything do to others as you would have them do to you."
>
> (Matthew 7:12)

The Golden Rule helps you make choices by putting yourself in the other person's place. How do your choices measure up?

 Cut out the Golden Rule and use it as a bookmark to remind yourself of how to measure your choices.

The Whole Law

One day, a man asked Jesus what he should do to live forever with God.

Jesus answered with another question: "What does God command of you in the law?" The man's answer is printed in the heart.

These words are the Great Commandment. They sum up the whole of God's law.

> "You shall love the Lord your God
> with all your heart,
> and with all your soul,
> and with all your strength,
> and with all your mind;
> and your neighbor
> as yourself."
>
> (Luke 10:27)

 Read the examples below. Write which kind of love each example represents: love for God, love for others, or love for yourself.

Praying to God _____

Playing with your little brother or sister _____

Going to church _____

Making Choices

Good moral choices don't just happen. You have to think about them. You have to practice making them. Most of all, you have to want to make good choices.

There are many reasons to want to make a good moral choice.

- You might want to avoid getting into trouble.
- You might want to please your family.

The best reason of all is to make the right choice out of love for yourself, for others, and for God.

Practice Makes Perfect

Practice the steps for making good moral choices shown here.

With a friend or family member, think of a situation you might face this week that would call for you to make a moral choice. Use this chart to help you practice the steps. Describe the situation, choices and consequences, and the best choice on the lines below.

_____

_____

_____

_____

_____

_____

_____

_____

Then

1. What are my choices in this situation?

Start here

2. What would the consequences of each choice be?

Then

3. What would Jesus choose?

4. What is the best choice?

Then

The Right Response

A *response* is something you say or do in answer to something someone else says or does. How would you respond in these situations?

Someone says, "Thank you." You say _____

_____

Someone tosses a ball to you. You _____

_____

Your friend looks really sad. You _____

_____

Response-Ability

When you make a moral choice, you are responsible for the consequences of your choice. You accept responsibility for what you choose and how it affects you and others.

When you make good choices, accepting responsibility means learning from your choices and repeating them. When you make bad choices, accepting responsibility means not making excuses or blaming others. You say you are sorry, do what you can to make up for what you have done, and promise to make better choices next time.

Circle the letter of the response that shows responsibility in each situation.

Choice	Responses
1. You choose to play a video game instead of finishing your homework.	**a.** You tell your teacher you were sick and couldn't finish your homework.
	b. You admit that you didn't finish your homework, and ask your teacher how you can make it up.
2. On Saturday, you choose to stay home and do extra chores to help your mom instead of going to the park with your friends.	**a.** You do more to help around the house during the next week, so chores don't have to wait until Saturday.
	b. The next time your mom asks for help, you tell her no. You say she owes you time with your friends.
3. You get so mad at your little sister that you break her favorite toy when she's not looking. When she finds it, she starts crying.	**a.** You tell her it was an accident and not to be such a baby.
	b. You admit that you broke her toy. You tell her you are sorry and offer to fix the toy or buy her a new one.

Be Welcoming

How can you tell that you are being welcomed? How can you tell when someone is shutting you out? The choice to be welcoming is a moral choice.

Decorate the Welcome Mat with signs of welcoming, belonging, and hospitality. Be sure to color in the letters.

Everyone Is Welcome

Jesus taught that everyone is welcome in God's Kingdom. Read the stories. Tell how you could make each person feel welcome.

People in Need of Welcoming	Ways You Can Be Welcoming
Rosa is a new girl in your class. On the playground you see her standing on the sidelines of your game. She looks like she wants to play, but she's too shy to ask.	
Your cousin is staying with your family while your aunt is in the hospital.	
Your mom is getting home tonight after a long business trip. Your dad has been working hard, too.	
The little kid down the street tags along to "help" you with your yard work and other chores, but gets in the way so much that it takes twice as long to get anything done.	

Be Just

"It's not fair!" How many times have you said this, or heard it said? So many things seem unfair. In a fair world, you might think that everyone would get exactly what he or she deserves.

Think of one unfair situation in your life. Tell a friend or family member how you would change things to make this situation fair.

You may wish for a fair world, but Jesus calls you to go beyond mere fairness. Jesus calls you to be just. Justice is more than fairness. In a just world, all people have what they need. All people stand up for one another. All people share. Here are some of the things Jesus said about being just.

> "If anyone wants to take your coat, give your cloak as well. Give to everyone who begs from you, and do not refuse anyone who wants to borrow from you." (Matthew 5:40,42)
>
> "Love your enemies, and pray for those who persecute you." (Matthew 5:44)
>
> Jesus told a story that compared God to an employer. The employer paid all his workers the same, whether they worked all day or only one hour. Jesus was saying that we should be like God—not just fair, but generous. (Matthew 20:1-16)

A Just World

Jesus calls you to imagine what a truly just world would be like. He wants you to act as though you live in such a world.

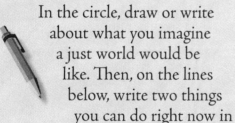

In the circle, draw or write about what you imagine a just world would be like. Then, on the lines below, write two things you can do right now in your life to be more just.

1. _____

2. _____

Be Forgiving

You've probably had many opportunities in your life to say you were sorry and to ask someone for forgiveness. You ask God's forgiveness, too, when you make wrong choices. But how often do you forgive others?

There's a connection between being forgiven and being forgiving. Use the key to decode these words about forgiveness from the Lord's Prayer:

___ ___ ___ ___ ___ ___ ___   ___ ___   ___ ___ ___   ___ ___ ___ ___ ___ ___ ___ ___ ___ ___ ___ ,
 3 8 10 4 6 14 2   13 11   8 13 10   12 10 2 11 9 1 11 11 2 11

___ ___   ___ ___   ___ ___ ___ ___ ___ ___ ___   ___ ___ ___ ___ ___   ___ ___ ___
 1 11   15 2   3 8 10 4 6 14 2   12 5 8 11 2   15 5 8

___ ___ ___ ___ ___ ___ ___ ___   ___ ___ ___ ___ ___ ___ ___ ___ ___ .
12 10 2 11 9 1 11 11   1 4 1 6 7 11 12 13 11

Code Key

1 = A	6 = I	11 = S
2 = E	7 = N	12 = T
3 = F	8 = O	13 = U
4 = G	9 = P	14 = V
5 = H	10 = R	15 = W

Forgiveness Central

Imagine you run a Web site about forgiveness. Read this e-mail. Respond with your advice on how to be forgiving.

Original message
To: Forgiveness Central
From: Steaming Stan

My sister took my favorite CD without asking, and she lost it. She offered to use her allowance to buy me a new one, but I'd rather get revenge by breaking her CD player.

To: Steaming Stan

_____

_____

_____

_____

_____

23

Help Those in Need

Mother Teresa lived among the poorest of the poor, caring for them and loving them. She said she saw Jesus in the face of every person in need. During her life, she was awarded the Nobel Peace Prize. Mother Teresa is remembered as an example of living a holy life. She was beatified, the first step to being declared a saint.

You are also called to help those in need. But you do not have to leave home or care for strangers. You do not have to win prizes. You do not even have to wait until you grow up. There are people in need waiting for your help, right here and right now.

God sends you and me to be his love to those who are in need.

Answering the Call

There are many ways to help those in need.

- Share food and drink with people who are hungry and thirsty.
- Make sure everyone has warm clothing.
- Visit people who are lonely.
- Care for people who are sick or hurt.
- Cheer up people who are sad.

In this space, tell how you can "be God's love" to someone who is hungry, thirsty, cold, lonely, sick, hurt, or sad. Make a promise to take action this week.

I can help someone who is _____

by _____

_____

I promise I will carry out my choice this week.

_____
Signature

With You Always

God is always with you. You can talk to God in prayer at any time, in any place. Did you know that prayer is also listening to God? God speaks to you in your mind and heart, through other people, and in the world around you.

Talking and Listening

Imagine yourself in each of these situations. Remember that God is with you. For each situation, think about what you would say to God. Then imagine what God would say to you.

Situation	What I would say to God	What God would say to me
You are just waking up on your birthday morning. You are looking forward to celebrating with your family and friends.		
You practiced really hard for your science report, but when you gave the report, you were very nervous. You skipped some important parts. Everyone applauded, but you still feel dumb.		
Your grandfather is in the hospital. Everybody seems really worried, but they won't answer your questions about how serious his illness is.		
You said a mean thing to your friend, and now no one will sit with you at the lunch table.		

Prayer of Praise

"What a great catch!"
  "You're an awesome singer!"
"I'm really proud of how your
  math grades improved!"
"You're the best!"

Everyone likes hearing words of praise like these. You might be praised for things that you do well or for trying hard. You might give praise to others when they shine at something special.

In each star, write some more words of praise you'd like to hear or share.

Praise and Glory

Prayer can be words of praise, too. In fact, prayers of praise are the purest form of prayer because you are not asking God for anything. You are simply honoring God for being God.

One name for the praise we give God is *glory*. A traditional prayer of praise gives glory to each of the persons of the Blessed Trinity. Catholics pray this prayer of praise during the Liturgy of the Hours and after each decade of the rosary. You can pray it anytime.

Fill in the blanks to complete the prayer.

Glory be to the _____,

and to the _____,

and to the _____ _____.

As it was in the _____,

is _____,

and ever shall be,

_____ _____ _____.

And that's a fact...

The prayer "Glory Be to the Father" is sometimes called a *doxology*. The name *doxology* is Greek for "words of praise."

The Lamb of God

What do you think of when you see a lamb?
What qualities do lambs have? Write down all the words you associate with a lamb.

_____   _____

_____   _____

Sometimes Jesus is called the Lamb of God to show just how much God loves his people.

When John the Baptist saw Jesus walking by the Jordan River, he said, here is the Lamb of God!" (John 1:29) John meant that Jesus was the Messiah promised by God to save everyone from sin.

Jesus, the Lamb of God, gave his life to save us. A man named John had a vision of heaven. He saw a lamb on a throne, surrounded by a whole crowd of saints praising God. (Revelation 5:6-11) The lamb on the throne is a sign of the risen Christ.

Grant Us Peace

At Mass, we pray or sing a prayer to Jesus, the Lamb of God, as the Bread of the Eucharist is broken to be shared. Learn this prayer so you can join in at Mass.

Lamb of God, you take away the sins of the world: have mercy on us.

Lamb of God, you take away the sins of the world: have mercy on us.

Lamb of God, you take away the sins of the world: grant us peace.

Draw your own symbol or write your own title for Jesus. Then compose your own short prayer to thank Jesus for bringing mercy and peace. Use the symbol or title in your prayer.

My symbol or title for Jesus   **My prayer**

Thanks for the Meal!

What is your favorite meal? Freshly baked pizza or your grandma's chicken soup? Vegetable lasagna? Baked apples from your uncle's tree? Homemade tamales? Hamburgers on the grill or fried chicken in a picnic basket? Pancakes on a lazy morning?

With a friend or family member, share your answers to these questions.

- What is the best dinner menu you can think of? List all the foods. _____

_____

- Who cooks or prepares these foods? _____

- Where do the ingredients come from before they get to the store? _____

_____

- Who would you want to share this meal with? _____

- Who cleans up? _____

Mealtime Prayers

Mealtime is a great time to pray. God is present at every meal, and you can give God thanks for the food, the people who grew and sold and prepared it, the people you are sharing the meal with, and the people who will clean up. You can also ask God to help people who are hungry and in need.

The prayer of thanks at meals is sometimes called *grace*, from the Latin word for "gifts." You can pray both before and after meals. Use traditional prayers or your own words.

Read the three meal prayers on these place mats. On the fourth place mat, write your own meal prayer.

Before Meals

Bless us, O Lord, and these your gifts which we are about to receive from your goodness, through Christ, our Lord. Amen.

After Meals

We give you thanks, for all your gifts, almighty God, living and reigning now and forever. Amen.

At Any Meal

Lord, give all people the food they need so they may join us in giving you thanks. Amen.

My Own Meal Prayer

All Day Long

God is always with you, so you can talk to God at any time of the day or night.

From Sunrise to Sunset

Many people like to start and end the day with prayer. You can use morning and evening prayers that others have written, or you can pray in your own words.

Color the windows to show the time of day. Read the morning and evening prayers. You can learn these by heart and use them when you want. Then, make up your own short prayers to use in the morning and at night.

A Morning Prayer

Almighty God,
fill my heart with your love
as morning fills the sky.
By living your law
may I have your peace in this life
and endless joy in the life to come.
Grant this through Christ our Lord.
Amen.

My Morning Prayer

An Evening Prayer

Heavenly Father,
may my evening prayer rise up to you,
and your blessing come down upon me.
May your help and salvation be mine
now and through all eternity.
I ask this in the name of Jesus the Lord.
Amen.

My Evening Prayer

Praying for Others

You know that you can ask God for anything you need. Prayer that asks something of God is called **petition**. But you can also ask God to help others. Prayer for others is called **intercession**.

- You can pray for people you know who are sick, or lonely, or sad.
- You can pray for people you don't know, in your own neighborhood or around the world, who are poor, or oppressed, or suffering from wars or natural disasters.
- You can even pray for people who have died, asking God to welcome them into his Kingdom.

On Sundays at Mass, the whole community prays for others in the **General Intercessions**, or the Prayer of the Faithful. We ask God to bless our community, our leaders, our country, people around the world, those who are in need, and those who have died. The Prayer of the Faithful is in the form of a **litany**. Another word for litany is *list*. A litany is a list of petitions, or asking prayers, to which everyone adds a repeated response. The usual response to the General Intercessions is "Lord, hear our prayer."

We Pray

Work with friends or family members to make up your own litany. Decide together what your response will be. Here are some possibilities:

- Lord, hear our prayer.
- Lord, have mercy.
- Hear us, O Lord.
- Help us, O God.

Let every person in your group make up one intention you could pray for:

- Your families
- Students and teachers in your school
- People in your parish or community
- People who are ill
- Places you have heard about in the news, where people are suffering from war, illness, terrorism, or natural disaster
- Those who have died

Take turns praying your petitions aloud. After each petition, pray the response together.

The Way of the Cross

Have you ever walked the Way of the Cross?

Long ago, people wanted to celebrate Lent and Holy Week by prayerfully following in Jesus' footsteps as he carried his cross. But the Holy Land was too far away, and travel was difficult and dangerous. So people walked the Way of the Cross in churches. They set up pictures or statues, called *stations*, to remind them of moments on Jesus' journey to Calvary. Some of these moments are described in the Bible. Others are based on what people imagined happened on the day Jesus died.

Your parish church may have stations of the cross that you can visit. Begin with the First Station. Look at the picture or statue, imagine you are there with Jesus, and say a short prayer. Move on to the next station, and repeat the process. Do this until you have visited all 14 stations.

Walking with Jesus

Even if your church does not have stations, you can still pray the Way of the Cross in your mind. Trace a path connecting all 14 stations of the cross. On the lines, write your own short prayer to repeat at each station. Use this page to help you pray the Way of the Cross any time.

1. Jesus is condemned to death.
2. Jesus takes up his cross.
3. Jesus falls the first time.
4. Jesus meets his sorrowful mother.
5. Simon of Cyrene helps Jesus carry the cross.
6. Veronica wipes the face of Jesus.
7. Jesus falls the second time.
8. The women of Jerusalem weep over Jesus.
9. Jesus is stripped of his garments.
10. Jesus falls the third time.
11. Jesus is nailed to the cross.
12. Jesus dies on the cross.
13. Jesus is taken down from the cross.
14. Jesus is laid in the tomb.

My Prayer for the Way of the Cross

Lord Jesus,

_____

_____

Amen.

Praying with God's Word

You can pray in the words of Scripture. Here are some prayers from the Bible you might use.

Mary's prayer of praise when she became the mother of Jesus:

"The Mighty One has done great things for me, and holy is his name."
(Luke 1:49)

A blind man's prayer to be healed:

"Jesus, Son of David, have mercy on me!" (Mark 10:47)

The prayer for forgiveness that Jesus taught his disciples:

"Father, hallowed be your name. Your kingdom come. Give us each day our daily bread. And forgive us our sins, for we ourselves forgive everyone indebted to us. And do not bring us to the time of trial." (Luke 11:1-4)

The Many Moods of Prayer

The Book of Psalms in the Bible is a whole collection of prayers. You can pray a psalm verse as a short prayer anytime. Read the psalm verses suggested here. Then look through the Book of Psalms yourself. Find psalm verses to pray for two other feelings or situations.

When you are happy or grateful . . .

"I will give thanks to the LORD with my whole heart." (Psalm 9:1)

When you need to make a decision . . .

"Make me to know your ways, O LORD; teach me your paths." (Psalm 25:4)

When you are afraid or hurting . . .

"O LORD, heal me, for my bones are shaking with terror." (Psalm 150:6)

Mood or situation: _____

Psalm verse: _____

Mood or situation: _____

Psalm verse: _____